DUNKLEOSTEUS

ANCIENT MARINE LIFE

BY KATE MOENING
ILLUSTRATIONS BY MAT EDWARDS

EPIC

BELLWETHER MEDIA • MINNEAPOLIS, MN

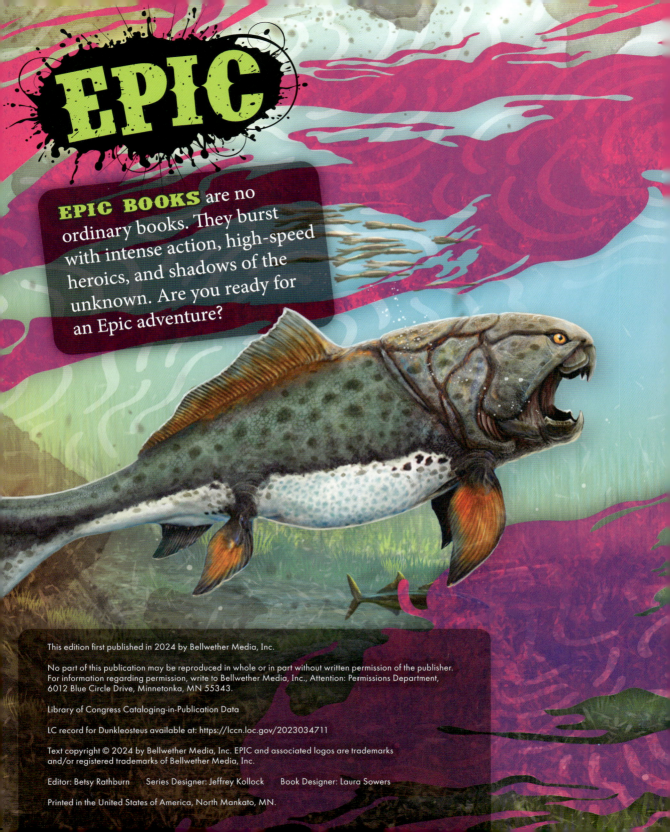

EPIC

EPIC BOOKS are no ordinary books. They burst with intense action, high-speed heroics, and shadows of the unknown. Are you ready for an Epic adventure?

This edition first published in 2024 by Bellwether Media, Inc.

No part of this publication may be reproduced in whole or in part without written permission of the publisher. For information regarding permission, write to Bellwether Media, Inc., Attention: Permissions Department, 6012 Blue Circle Drive, Minnetonka, MN 55343.

Library of Congress Cataloging-in-Publication Data

LC record for Dunkleosteus available at: https://lccn.loc.gov/2023034711

Text copyright © 2024 by Bellwether Media, Inc. EPIC and associated logos are trademarks and/or registered trademarks of Bellwether Media, Inc.

Editor: Betsy Rathburn   Series Designer: Jeffrey Kollock   Book Designer: Laura Sowers

Printed in the United States of America, North Mankato, MN.

TABLE OF CONTENTS

WHAT WAS THE DUNKLEOSTEUS?	4
THE LIFE OF THE DUNKLEOSTEUS	10
FOSSILS AND EXTINCTION	16
GET TO KNOW THE DUNKLEOSTEUS	20
GLOSSARY	22
TO LEARN MORE	23
INDEX	24

WHAT WAS THE DUNKLEOSTEUS?

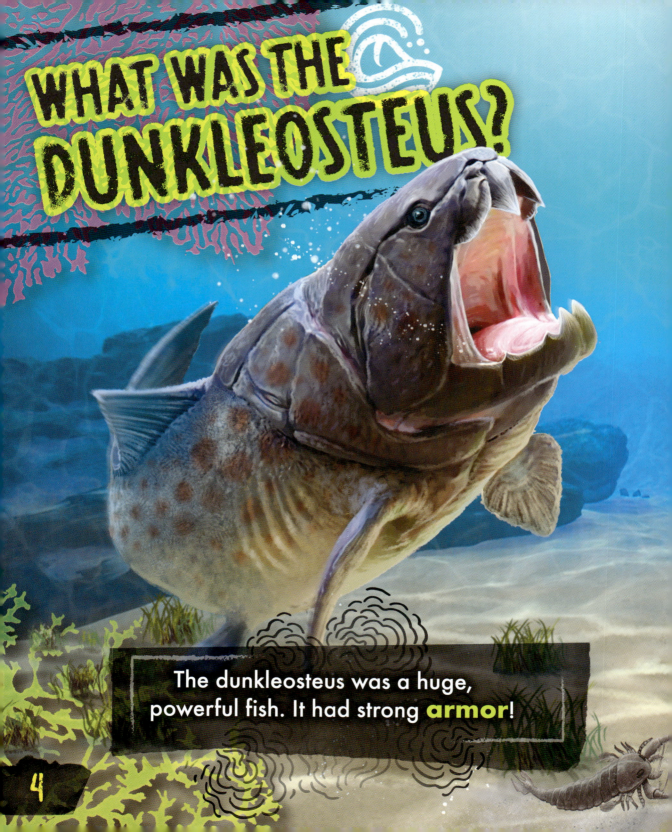

The dunkleosteus was a huge, powerful fish. It had strong **armor**!

4

MAP OF THE WORLD

Late Devonian period

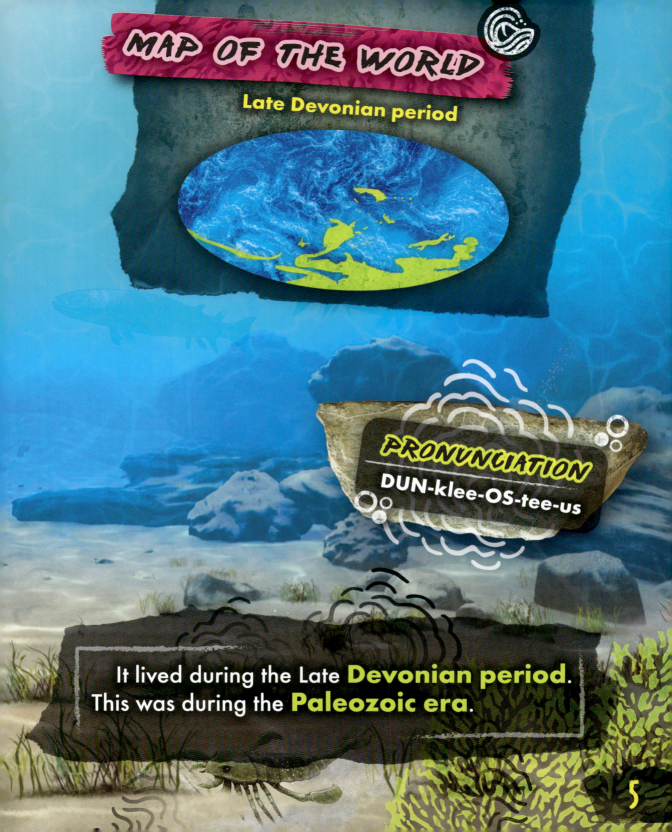

PRONUNCIATION
DUN-klee-OS-tee-us

It lived during the Late **Devonian period**. This was during the **Paleozoic era**.

The dunkleosteus grew to around 13 feet (4 meters) long. It weighed over 2,000 pounds (907 kilograms).

Its body was thick and strong. This fish was a powerful swimmer!

SIZE COMPARISON

about as long as an SUV

The dunkleosteus did not have teeth. But its jaws had sharp points. They cut through **prey** like scissors!

jaw

The fish also had huge muscles in its jaws. These gave it a powerful bite!

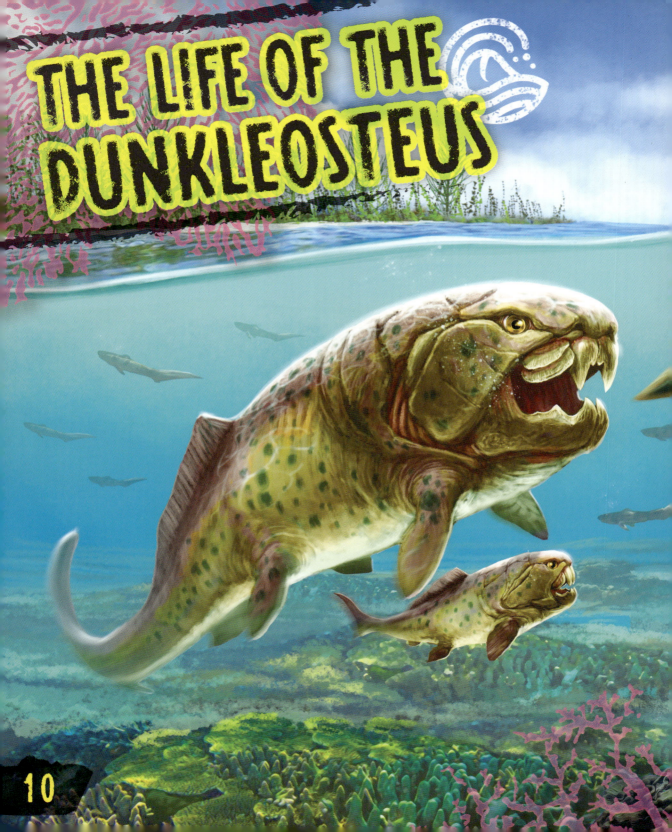

Earth's **continents** were once much closer together. There was a **shallow** ocean between what is now North America and Africa.

Many animals lived here. The dunkleosteus lived here, too. It likely spent its time alone.

The dunkleosteus was an **apex predator**. It ate fish, sharks, and even other dunkleosteus! Its huge jaws moved very fast. This helped suck in a lot of food at once!

SPEED EATER
The dunkleosteus ate quickly. It could open and close its jaws more than 10 times per second!

DUNKLEOSTEUS DIET

fish

sharks

dunkleosteus

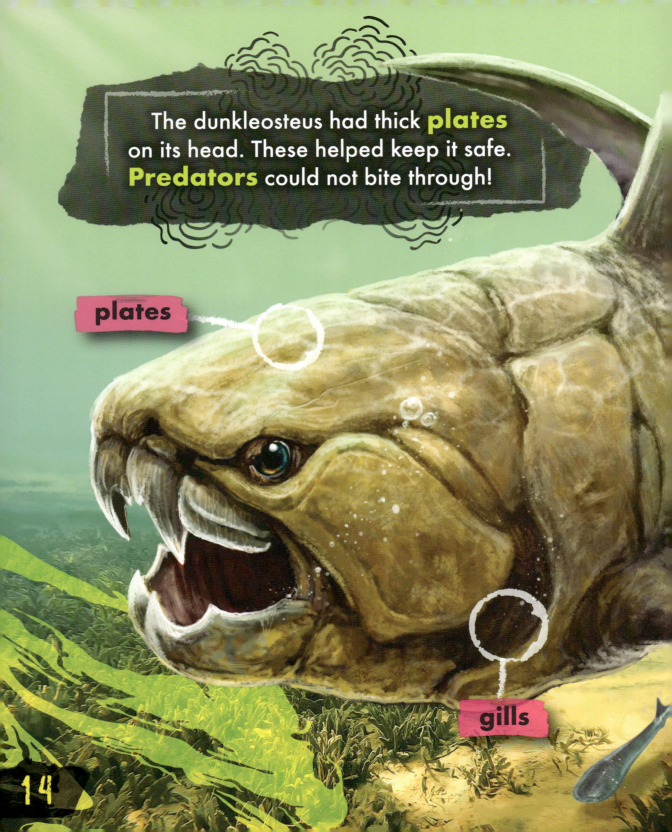

But the fish's **gills** were less protected. Bigger fish could take a bite!

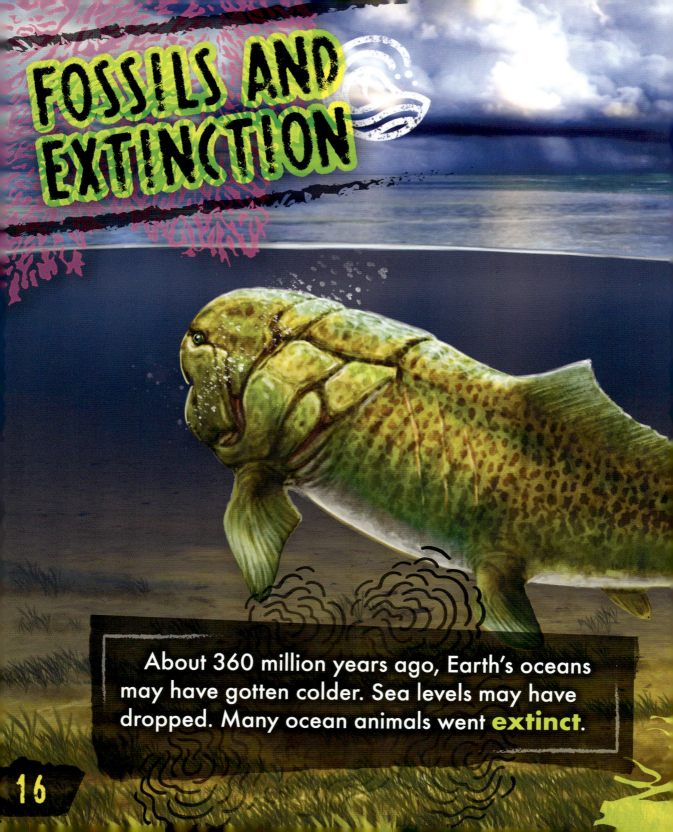

FOSSILS AND EXTINCTION

About 360 million years ago, Earth's oceans may have gotten colder. Sea levels may have dropped. Many ocean animals went **extinct**.

The dunkleosteus did not survive the changes. It went extinct, too.

The first dunkleosteus **fossil** was found in Ohio in 1867.

fossil

NO BODY

The dunkleosteus's only bones were on its head. There are no fossils of other parts. Scientists can only guess what its body looked like!

LARGEST COMPLETE DUNKLEOSTEUS SKULL

model of dunkleosteus skull

FOUND 1928

LOCATED Cuyahoga County, Ohio

More fossils have been found around the world. There is still more to learn about this fearsome predator!

19

GET TO KNOW THE DUNKLEOSTEUS

FIRST FOSSIL FOUND
Jay Terrell and later by David Dunkle

LOCATION
oceans between what is now North America, northern Africa, Europe, and western Asia

SIZE
around 13 feet (4 meters) long

GLOSSARY

apex predator—an animal at the top of the food chain that is not preyed upon by other animals

armor—a hard covering that protects an animal

continents—the seven major land areas on Earth

Devonian period—the fourth period of the Paleozoic era that occurred between 419 million and 359 million years ago.

extinct—no longer living

fossil—the remains of a living thing that lived long ago

gills—openings along the side of the head that the dunkleosteus used for breathing

Paleozoic era—a time in history that happened about 541 million to 252 million years ago; many new kinds of ocean life appeared during the Paleozoic era.

plates—flat, hard pieces that cover the bodies of some animals

predators—animals that hunt other animals for food

prey—animals that are hunted by other animals for food

shallow—not very deep

TO LEARN MORE

AT THE LIBRARY

Garrod, Ben. *Extinct: Dunkleosteus*. London, U.K.: Head of Zeus, 2021.

Hall, Ashley. *Fossils for Kids: A Junior Scientist's Guide to Dinosaur Bones, Ancient Animals, and Prehistoric Life on Earth.* Emeryville, Calif.: Rockridge Press, 2020.

Walker, Alan. *Fossils and Sea Animals*. New York, N.Y.: Crabtree Publishing Company, 2022.

ON THE WEB

Factsurfer.com gives you a safe, fun way to find more information.

1. Go to www.factsurfer.com.

2. Enter "dunkleosteus" into the search box and click 🔍.

3. Select your book cover to see a list of related content.

Index

Africa, 11
apex predator, 12
armor, 4
bite, 9, 14, 15
body, 7, 18
bones, 18
continents, 11
Earth, 11, 16
extinct, 16, 17
fish, 4, 7, 9, 12, 15
food, 12, 13
fossil, 18, 19
get to know, 20–21
gills, 14, 15

jaws, 8, 9, 12, 13
Late Devonian period, 5
map, 5, 19
muscles, 9
North America, 11
oceans, 11, 16
Ohio, 18, 19
Paleozoic era, 5
plates, 14
predators, 14, 15, 19
prey, 8, 12, 13
pronunciation, 5
scientists, 18
size, 6, 7

The images in this book are reproduced through the courtesy of: Mat Edwards, front cover, pp. 1, 2-3, 4-5, 6-7, 8-9, 10-11, 12-13, 14-15, 16-17, 18-19, 20-21; Zachi Evenor/ Wikipedia, p. 19 (model).